AF338274

Bethlehem: The House of Bread

Bethlehem: The House of Bread

The Biblical Case for the Eucharist

James S. Anderson

WIPF & STOCK · Eugene, Oregon

BETHLEHEM: THE HOUSE OF BREAD
The Biblical Case for the Eucharist

Wipf & Stock
An Imprint of Wipf and Stock Publishers
199 W. 8th Ave., Suite 3
Eugene, OR 97401

www.wipfandstock.com

PAPERBACK ISBN: 978-1-6667-8952-2
HARDCOVER ISBN: 978-1-6667-8953-9
EBOOK ISBN: 978-1-6667-8954-6

VERSION NUMBER 10/16/23

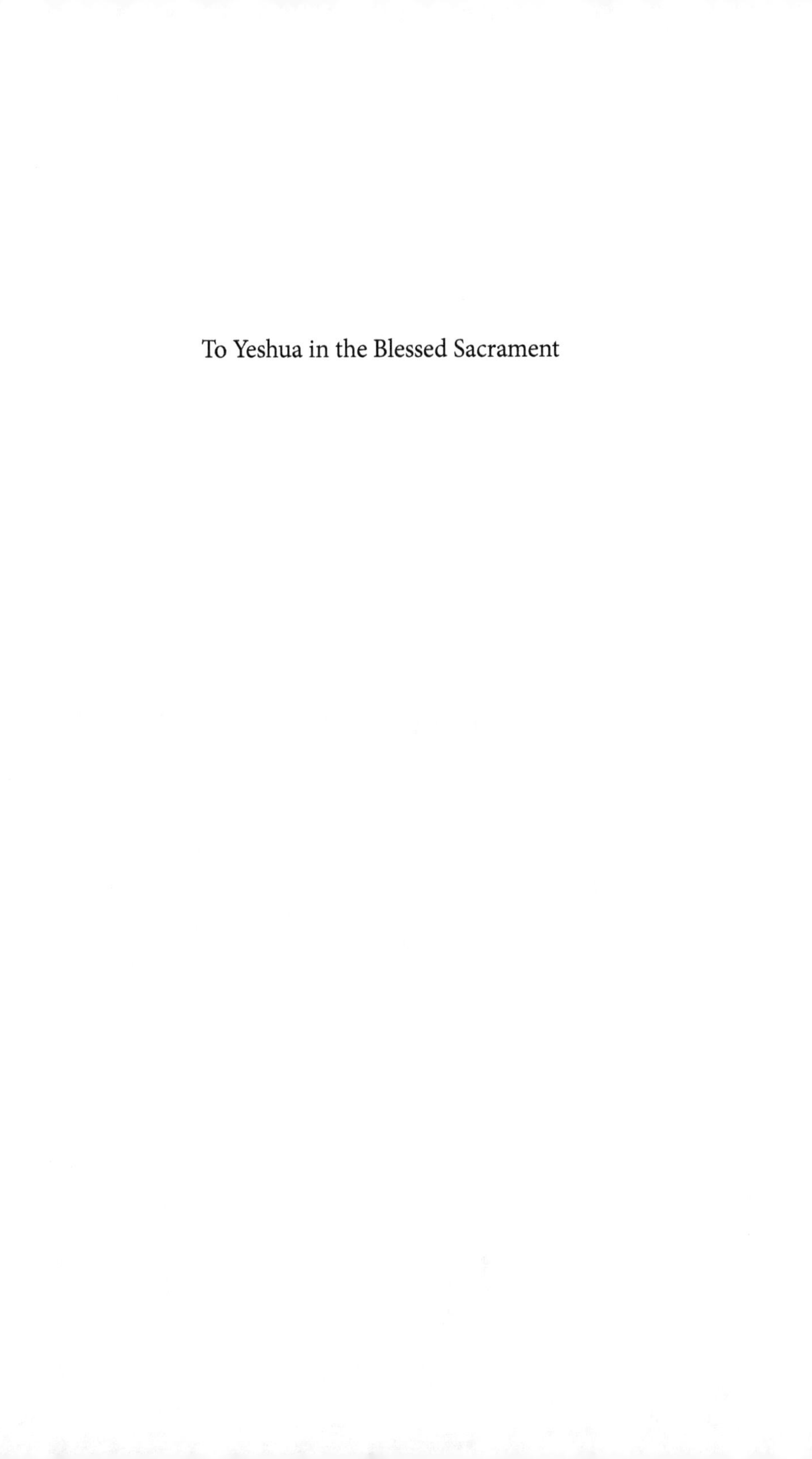

To Yeshua in the Blessed Sacrament

Contents

CONTENTS

Abbreviations

CCC   *Catechism of the Catholic Church.* (2nd edition, Vatican: Libreria Editrice Vaticana, 2012).

SC   Second Vatican Council, Constitution on the Sacred Liturgy Sacrosanctum Concilium in *Vatican Council II: The Conciliar and Post Conciliar Documents.* Edited by Austin Flannery (Collegeville, MN: Liturgical Press, 1975).

Introduction

At the Last Supper, on the night he was betrayed, our Savior instituted the Eucharistic sacrifice of his Body and Blood. This he did in order to perpetuate the sacrifice of the cross throughout the ages until he should come again, and so to entrust to his beloved Spouse, the Church, a memorial of his death and resurrection: a sacrament of love, a sign of unity, a bond of charity, a Pascal banquet in which Christ is consumed, the mind is filled with grace, and a pledge of future glory is given to us.[1]

Like many American Christians today, I previously thought the Catholic teaching on the Eucharist bizarre at best, ridiculous at worst. Recent polls suggest that over eighty percent of Catholics in this country do not believe in the Real Presence of Christ in the Eucharist. They thus ignore the consistent teaching of the Church rooted in the writings of the Church Fathers who had no doubt about the Real Presence of Christ in the Eucharist.

Since its inception, the Church has always maintained that Jesus is really, truly, and substantially present in the most holy sacrament of the Eucharist. In the Gospels, Jesus commands us to partake of it and doing so can transform one's life. In this, Jesus was himself faithful to the teachings of the Hebrew Scriptures, the Bible of his days. This is in a nutshell the argument of this booklet: the sacrament of the Eucharist is thoroughly biblical, not merely a weird doctrine based on the New Testament, but a truly biblical

1. SC §47; CCC §1323.

teaching founded on both the Old and the New Testament. Such a claim will surprise many, particularly Protestants, who have been taught that Christ is really and substantially present in the Eucharist is a medieval innovation that has no biblical roots.

As the real presence of Christ was one of the main doctrines over which the Western Church split, would it not be wiser to leave such a controversial issue, all the more so since many Catholics do not understand it, or understand it but remain incredulous? If, however, the holy sacrament of the Eucharist truly goes all the way back to Jesus who taught it in accordance to his Bible, i.e., the Hebrew Scriptures or the Old Testament as Christians call it somewhat derogatorily, there is serious ground to reconsider this doctrine.

Following the example of the early church, the Second Vatican Council declared taking part in the Eucharistic sacrifice the "fount and apex" (i.e., the source and summit) of the Christian life.[2] If so, all Catholics ought to take at least a few moments to reflect on the source and summit of their faith. If, as is argued below, the Eucharist is based upon both the New and the Old Testaments, even Protestants ought to reconsider the issue that has been blurred by the heat of sixteenth century controversies that tore the Western Church apart.

There are seven sacraments in the Catholic Church, seven as the seven days of creation in Genesis, a symbol of wholeness or completeness. It is therefore fitting that these seven sacraments "are efficacious signs of grace, instituted by Christ and entrusted to the Church, by which divine life is dispensed to us"..[3] Our Protestant brothers and sisters only have two sacraments, baptism and communion. Catholics do not view Protestant communion as a valid Eucharist because it takes a valid priest of the Church to preside over it and confect it.

Moreover, the Sacrament of the Holy Eucharist is intimately related to the Sacrament of Reconciliation, while both sacraments participate actively in the healing of soul, mind, and body. Healing

2. Vatican II, "Lumen Gentium," §11; CCC §1324.

3. CCC §1131.

deep spiritual or psychological issues often heals physical ones that are related since, as the Church teaches, we are both body and spirit.[4] The fourth or fifth century Book of Masses from Toledo in modern-day Spain implores God that those who receive the Eucharist "might draw from it salvation and the healing of soul and body."[5] The transforming potential of the Catholic sacramental economy is reason enough to consider the Eucharist afresh.

4. CCC §365; see Schuchts, *Healed.*
5. "Post Pridie" in Cabie, *History,* 26

The Real Presence of Christ in the Eucharist

Historical Overview

T he Church has always taught that the Eucharist is the body and blood of Christ, that is, the Real Presence. After Vatican II the dimension of sacrifice was downplayed to emphasize the sharing of a sacred meal. Nevertheless, at every Mass the once and for all sacrifice of Christ on the cross is extended across time and space to us. The Eucharist is a representation of Christ's sacrifice. We join our sacrifice to it and offer it back to God. Its sacrificial dimension in recent years has come back to prominence.

It has only been within the last five hundred years that the Real Presence of Christ in the elements of the bread and wine transformed by the Holy Spirit at Mass was challenged.[1] As heresy often does, the Protestant challenge spurred the Church to refine and better articulate its position on the Real Presence of Christ in the Eucharist.

It is of one of the Church's greatest saint, Thomas Aquinas, who provided the foundation for how we articulate the Eucharist today. Aquinas presided over Mass twice a day and is said to have synthesized Christianity with Aristotelian philosophy not from study but from laying his head upon the tabernacle that housed

1. CCC §1105.

the Eucharist. Regrettably, the Eucharist has become a source of division, though this is hardly surprising.

Jesus, or Yeshua as was his Aramaic name (both names will be used), himself was aware that his message to a distorted world would inevitably generate strife. According to his own words, he did not come to bring peace but division, setting a man against his father, a daughter against her mother, and a daughter-in-law against her mother-in-law" (Matt 10:35; Luke 12:52). The Eucharist has been and continues to be a fault line within Christianity. Catholic and Eastern Orthodox brothers and sisters do share the same faith in the Eucharist, but once schism ensues, reconciliation it is very hard to obtain. This little guide recaptures biblical roots of the gift of grace flowing to us from Yeshua's work on the cross in the Eucharist.

The House of Bread

Part of the title of this booklet, *House of Bread,* derives form the name of Yeshua's birthplace, Bethlehem. In Hebrew, Bethlehem means "house" or "temple" of "bread." As Yeshua referred to the temple of his body that would be raised from the dead (John 2:19), it is appropriate seeing Yeshua as our temple of bread from which originate the bread that we eat at the celebration of the Eucharist.

This booklet is for anyone who has eyes to see and read what is written in our Holy Bible. It points to what has the power to save. Simply put: partaking of the Eucharist is nothing less that taking in Yeshua himself. As much as baptism, the Eucharist is foundational to a Christian and it is most worthy to reflect on it more here.

As some of us cannot take the wine because of health issues, the Church teaches that one only need one of the species, either bread or wine to engage in the full, real presence of Christ in the Eucharist. Therefore taking only the body of Yeshua is enough to partake of the entire Eucharist, according to Church teaching. The blood does not also have to be taken. Please note here I say body and blood, for that is what they are after consecration. They are no longer bread and wine, but the sacred mysteries are both truly, really, fully, and substantially Christ—body, mind, and soul—thus the Eucharist at Mass. Jesus is still with us today in a more special way every time we celebrate the Mass.

What follows is not an exhaustive treatment of the topic nor a scholarly one. It simply shows how the Eucharist and more specifically the Real Presence of Christ in it is thoroughly biblical, logically following the teachings of the Church, of Yeshua, and of the great figures of the "Old" Testament.

The Eucharist in Short

Staying away from Mass and the Eucharist is missing out on the gift and grace of God. Miraculous events and healings often occur when taking the Eucharist at Mass or praying before it at Adoration. Healing, however, occurs more often in a slow, incremental transformation by continued practice and partaking of the Eucharist worthily.[2]

Partaking of the Eucharist worthily essentially means one is not aware of unconfessed mortal sins. Mortal sins need to be confessed, whereas venial sins are taken care of or forgiven at every Mass. One might object to classifying sins as venial or mortal; however, some sins are obviously worse than others. Though all wrongdoing is sin, all sins are not mortal (1 John 5:17). Therefore, others are indeed mortal. They bear on one's eternal well-being and need to be atoned for by Christ. The lists of sins in Gal 5:19–21 and Rom 1:28–32 do not establish a clear distinction between mortal and venial sins. The Church does not have a specific list of mortal sins either; nevertheless, breaking the Ten Commandments are usually considered mortal sins, with adultery, fornication, and blasphemy, among others. The Church provides the sacrament of reconciliation to free us from the burden of our sins.

Suffering is ubiquitous in this life. As Christians, we are not called to run away from suffering, but to address it, for it is a part of life, not an aberration. We seek to alleviate it in others, wherever we

2. Radcliffe, *Drama*, 6.

find it, and in ourselves when possible, joining it to Christ's suffering on the cross. We always seek to turn suffering into redemptive suffering. This is exactly what the Eucharist helps us achieve as we approach the passion of the "physician of souls and bodies".[3]

Yeshua promises that whoever eats his flesh and drinks his blood has eternal life, and will be raised on the last day" (John 6:53–54). As we continue to partake in the Eucharist as he commands us, we demonstrate our faith in God for "to believe in him and to receive his Body become one and the same action."[4]

Two Fundamental Questions

There are two fundamental questions every person must ask themselves. The first comes from Yeshua himself, as recorded in the gospels and thus reverberates to us today. Before setting off for his last journey to Jerusalem, Yeshua asks his disciples: "Who do you say I am?" (Matt 16:13–20; Mark 8:27–30; Luke 9:18–21; John 6:67–71). The second question follows from how one answers the first: "How can this man give us his flesh to eat?" (John 6:52)

Peter, the first Pope of the Church, gets the first question right as he exclaims, "You are the Messiah, the Son of the living God." And Yeshua adds that it was not by his own accord he knew the answer but that it is God in heaven who made this known to him (Matt 16:17).

To answer as Peter did is to believe in Yeshua as Christ and thus to be a Christian. This is not to deny that one needs be baptized to be brought into the Church of Christ. Yet, to be part of the body of Christ, one does not necessarily have to be Catholic. God's grace and the body of Christ no doubt extends beyond the Church, though the Catholic Church is the fullness of the faith.[5] While the invisible Church is known by God and exists widely, the Catholic Church makes visible a part of the invisible church.

3. CCC §1509.

4. Levering and Dauphinais, *Wisdom*, 120.

5. Vatican II, "Nostra Aetate."

The first question—"Who do you say I am?"—is answered in faith, faith granted by God, itself a gift not merited by us, something over which Catholics and Protestants agree.

The majority in America today, including Catholics, have missed the second question: "How can this man give us his flesh to eat?" If one understands Yeshua to be the Son of God, one must also ask what is the Eucharist. Is it a mere symbolic act or the very body and blood of Jesus John 6 commands us to eat? How one answers this question impacts how one lives and whether or not one actually partakes of God's grace, literally.

A caveat is in order here. Many worthy Christians throughout the ages who no doubt are with God missed out on this grace, though taking part in the Eucharist is the source and summit of the Christian life.[6] Many were our Protestant brothers and sisters, and many were Catholics who for hundreds of years were not given the Eucharist in the Church because only the clergy received it.

How one answers the first question addresses essentially whether or not one is a Christian, a believer in Christ, and the latter tells what type of Christian we are. How one answers the latter question impacts not only the way we worship, but from a Catholic view, it impacts and effects the amount of help and literal grace we receive in this life, which impacts both our spiritual and physical well-being.[7] No wonder the Church requires Mass attendance every Sunday, not as a rule to follow but as a healing balm, much akin to commanding someone to take medicine that will make them well. It also fulfills the commandment to honor the Sabbath, the Church's Sabbath. According to Catholic tradition and theology, the once-for-all sacrifice of Yeshua on the cross extends across time and place to benefit those who partake it worthily. Having proclaimed that "unless you eat my flesh and drink my blood no life is in you," Yeshua adds "Those who eat my flesh and drink my blood have eternal life, and I will raise them up on the last day" (John 6:53–54). This is indeed profound.

6. Vatican II, "Lumen Gentium," §11.

7. CCC §1509; 1 Cor 11:30; John 6:54.

One can answer the first question correctly and be part of Christ's body the Church, but missing the second question misses out on what Yeshua instituted to allow the Church to fully partake of his grace in this life that flows from his work on the cross. Consequently, one misses out on the fullness of the faith. That is why Vatican II called the Eucharist the source and summit of the Christian life.[8] Profound implications follow from our answers to these two questions.

Against a common Protestant claim that the Catholic Mass and Eucharist is a re-sacrifice of Yeshua, the Eucharist is a representation in any particular time and place of the once for all sacrifice of Yeshua that occurred on the cross at Golgotha in first-century Palestine. This is possible as God stands outside time and space, and can thus make possible this extension of his sacrifice and grace. How God becomes present in a piece of bread and a little wine is certainly a deep mystery, but when he does, it is no longer bread and wine, but the body and soul of Yeshua. Only God can do so. His ways are not our ways (Isa 55:8), but this is his way of conferring his grace to us. This is the mystery by which he comes to us in the bread and wine after consecration at the Mass.

Undoubtedly, this teaching has always have been a stumbling block to many and continues to be so.[9] When Yeshua explained that whoever eats his flesh and drinks his blood has eternal life, the Jews wondered "how can this man give us his flesh to eat?" (John 6:52). Even his disciples considered this teaching difficult and many turned away (John 6:60–66). He let them walk away, not trying to soften his teaching by arguing that is merely a metaphor!

Therefore, the two questions posed here are pivotal. 1) "Who do you say that I am?" And 2) what do you think the Eucharist is? These two questions are inextricably intertwined for to believe in him and to receive his Body become one and the same.

8. Vatican II, "Lumen Gentium," §11.
9. CCC §1336.

The Mass and the Eucharist

The term "Mass" derives from the Latin formula *"ite missa est"* that closes the service; the term *missa* means "to be sent." The term "Eucharist" derives from the Greek term *eucharistia*, meaning thanksgiving. One is sent into the world as leaven after the thanksgiving to God that has occurred at the Mass. The focal point of the Mass is the Eucharist. In the liturgy we lift our hearts and minds to God to offer Him our praise. We join in the work of God and the church in the sacred liturgy. The Mass is also a sacrifice. We give back our gifts to God. That is why before the elements are consecrated by invoking the Holy Spirit, when the celebrant stands at the altar over the elements and prays to God on behalf of the people, the priest prays, "Pray, brethren, that my sacrifice and yours be acceptable to God, the almighty Father."

For good reason every Sunday is a holy day of obligation, for by attending Sunday Mass, we fulfill the command of keeping the Sabbath holy, not to mention it nourishes and feeds the people of God as they journey throughout the week. We now fulfill the commandment on Sunday rather than on Saturday, the day of the Jewish Sabbath, because the church shifted it to the day in which Jesus rose from the dead (Matt 16:19). In going to Mass, we join with those in heaven worshipping God. In this sense, the Mass provides a glimpse of the heavenly liturgy (Rev 5:8–11) and grants its participants the privilege of being mystically joined with all those who before us have done the same. In his *Spiritual Diary*, St. Ignatius of Loyola, the creator of the Spiritual Exercises, stressed how vital it is to attend Mass and partake of the Eucharist daily. This is integral for practicing his discernment of spirits.[10]

The Mass has always comprised the Liturgy of Word followed by the Liturgy of Eucharist. This can be seen already in the work of the second-century Church father, Justin Martyr, who details the rubrics of the Mass. The first part of the Mass contains the reading of Scripture followed by a homily making the readings from Scripture relevant for today. It orients the people to the Word of God

10. Gallagher, *Will*, 50.

and God's teachings. Undoubtedly, God can and does speak to us through the liturgy of the Word, through the reading of the Bible and the proclamation of his sacred Scriptures. This point in the service is the focal point in most Protestant traditions. The focal point of the Catholic Mass follows with the liturgy of the Eucharist. The Mass today occurs for the same reason the early Church gathered—to celebrate the Eucharist. The Mass then is thoroughly biblical.[11] Additionally, all the prayers, gestures, and proclamations—including the reciting of the Creed—have deep biblical underpinnings and significance, as the response of the people is often a direct quotation from Scripture.

The Eucharist is the central mystery of the faith and most Church Fathers argue that it is the most important of the seven sacraments. No doubt the Mass has evolved throughout the ages, but it began with the early church gathering to celebrate the Eucharist. The writings of Justin Martyr as much as the early document known as the Didache, both from the second century, show how the Mass contained essentially the same rubrics used today. The Didache makes apparent that the early church clearly gathered for the primary purpose of celebrating the sacred mysteries.

During the liturgy of the Eucharist, the priest offers prayers and approaches the altar to implore the Holy Spirit to effect the change of the bread and wine into the body and blood of Christ. When he pronounces the words of consecration, the priest acts in *persona Christi* ("in the person of Christ"). When he raises the bread and later the wine and quotes the very words of Yeshua from the Last Supper saying, "this is my body" and later "this is my blood of the new and eternal covenant" (see Jer 31:31) the change occurs to the respective elements. It is the Holy Spirit who effects the change. It is by Yeshua's very words through the priest acting in *persona Christi* that the elements are transformed and become the body and blood of Christ, not mere symbols. As Yeshua did, the priest says this *is* his body and blood. We take his words at face value, for no falsehood is found in Jesus.

11. Sri, *Walk*, 1–4.

Therefore, a "most amazing event in the universe takes place at every Mass: The Son of God himself comes upon our altars and dwells in our midst!"[12] The food we are given is the healing balm of his presence. It contains all we need for the journey of our life. Thus, "the Eucharist is the sum and summary of our faith".[13]

The Eucharist as Sacrifice

Yeshua's work on the cross continues to work in the Eucharist, to give us his saving grace in the present. It has been the consistent teaching of the Church that the Mass is to be understood as a sacrifice. This teaching goes back to the last book of the Minor Prophets in the Old Testament, which announces that the Gentiles will offer "a pure offering in every place" (Mal 1:11). The Apostle Paul refers to the Eucharistic table as an altar, which implies a sacrifice offered to God (1 Cor 9:13). Thus, the Eucharistic celebration should be understood as a sacrifice.

At the Mass:

> The Father's love for his Son Jesus extends to us too as he offers us the same sacrifice of his son in the Eucharist. We offer that same sacrifice back to the Father with the plea that he would accept us through his Son. We can be reconciled to God only through Christ's sacrifice. For this reason, our worship today must contain the same sacrifice if we are to continue to be acceptable to the Father.[14]

Without such a sacrifice, we are not truly worshipping God. Before the destruction of their temples, the Jews worshipped God by offering sacrifices. Consequently, the Eucharist is a *sacrifice* offered on every consecrated altar across the world. If not, Christians presume to approach God without due respect, "empty-handed," something Deuteronomy 16:16 prohibits. It is the sacrifice offered at the Mass that makes our worship acceptable to

12. Sri, *Walk*, 11.

13. CCC §1327.

14. Howell, *Eucharist*, 58.

God, though it is crucial to understand that it does not sacrifice Yeshua again but makes present—rather than represents—the once-and-for all sacrifice of Christ for anyone partaking of the Eucharist. This is not a mere memorial. In the Eucharist, Christ is present among us and in us.

The Eucharist is the summit of the faith and the culmination of the Mass. The liturgy of the Word that precedes it in the Mass is important as well, though homilies should not be too long. Ultimately, the Eucharist is a profound mystery of the faith. We receive the bread and wine of the Eucharist as the Real Presence of Jesus as did all Christians at the very beginning of the Church. It is therefore appropriate that after the liturgy of the Word and during the liturgy of the Eucharist, the priest pronounces after the words of consecration: "the mystery of the faith."

The three salient aspects regarding the Eucharist celebrated at Mass are 1) Sacrifice made present, 2) Communal meal, and 3) Real Presence.

The Mass is above all a sacrifice offered in which Yeshua is not re-sacrificed but rather present across time and space. Yeshua's sacrifice from the past becomes present as we join our sacrifice to it and give it back to God. It is therefore God's sacrifice along with ours.

We also commune with each other in the sacred meal of communion, or the Eucharist, precisely because, according to another vital principle of the Church given to us by Paul again, at Baptism we are joined into one body (1 Cor 12:13). Though Paul uses the metaphor of the body, it is more than just a metaphor for Christians. We actually take the body imagery literally. We are part of the one body of Yeshua and thus the Church is Yeshua in the world. Recall Galatians 3:28: "There is no longer Jew or Greek, there is no longer slave or free, there is no longer male and female; for all of you are one in Christ Jesus." To take in the Eucharist is to become one in Christ Jesus with all the others who too are coming to him in the Eucharist and taking him into their bodily temples.

Christ is the head of the body and each individual Christian is a different and unique part of his body. We all participate in

Jesus in a very real way. At Mass we take Jesus into our body and all share in his body. By implication, when one member of the body hurts, we all hurt. When one does well, we all do.

Finally, the Real Presence of Christ in the Eucharist is the truth of the Church. Thus, regarding the Mass:

> The entire Pascal Mystery of Jesus' passion death and resurrection is made present to us in the Eucharistic Liturgy so that we can be more deeply incorporated into Jesus' life and mission. The more deeply the Eucharist unites us to Jesus, the more we will radiate his life and love in the world around us.[15]

It is appropriate at this point to turn briefly to two modern-day giants in American Catholicism today. Both are role models and have been involved in educating people and offer much on the topic at hand. Though they would both be uneasy with such lauding, they have opened the eyes of many on the subject. One is a former Presbyterian minister and convert to Catholicism, now a professor at Franciscan University of Steubenville, the other ministers to thousands online and via social media. The first is Professor Scott Hahn and the other is Bishop Robert Barron.

Scott Hahn

Scott Hahn is a most influential Catholic in America today.[16] His 1999 popular book *The Lamb's Supper* presents the book of Revelation as a blueprint for the Mass and vice versa. To this aim, he reads the book of Revelation symbolically because it does not lay out the Mass as it progresses in a linear fashion any more than it can be read as a map for how the world comes to an end. In fact, the world destroys itself several times over in Revelation. Read symbolically, however, Revelation indeed portrays those in heaven worshiping the Lord, just as is done in the divine liturgy. In the Mass we join those in heaven in such worship.

15. Sri, *Walk*, 148.

16. Martin, *American Pope*.

The Last Supper was a Passover meal by which Yeshua established the new covenant by his blood. The first Mass occurred at the Last Supper; this was the first time people feasted on the Eucharist. So the institution of the Mass on the night Yeshua celebrated Passover with his disciples at the Last Supper is a sacrifice in which he instituted the New Covenant of the Eucharist. It will be seen below how this New Covenant was commanded in the Book of Deuteronomy and prophesied about long before Yeshua by the prophet Jeremiah, a covenant that would also be a circumcision of the heart and offered to all of humanity. At the Last Supper, Yeshua not only reveals he is the new Passover instituting a new exodus with its communal meal, but he too invokes the words of the prophet Jeremiah (Jer 31:31–34) revealing he is the New Covenant. The Eucharist is the New Covenant because it encapsulates Yeshua and his sacrifice. Hahn explains that when on the cross Yeshua cried out "It is finished," at that very moment the Passover ritual was complete because he drunk the forth cup handed over to him via a hyssop branch.[17] This branch is reminiscent of the branch prescribed to sprinkle the lamb's blood on lintels and doorposts during the Passover ritual (Exod 12:22).

Bishop Robert Barron

Bishop Robert Barron is becoming the face of American Catholicism, the new Fulton J. Sheen. He is the founder of the rapidly growing apostolate *Word on Fire*. Its aim has been to evangelize and catechize the young unaffiliated in this country, the so called "nones." *Word on Fire* hosts a website, articles, a publishing house, podcasts, debates, resources for parishes and boasts over a thousand YouTube videos on topics related to Catholicism, making content accessible and relevant to a vast array of people today. His award-wining *Catholicism: The Pivotal Players* videos are inspiring and the production value impressive. His not-dumbing-down the faith approach is refreshing and timely. He is an erudite

17. Hahn, *Fourth Cup*, 113–16.

scholar who, by his own account, has spent the last 20 years evangelizing the culture to counter pernicious moral relativism and the rise of the so-called New Atheists.

Barron republished an important treatment of our topic through *Word on Fire* appropriately entitled, *Eucharist*. In it, Barron details the salient aspects of the Eucharist—sacrifice, Real Presence, and communal meal. By way of making use of the Danish short story "Babetts's Feast" published in 1956, he analyzes the biblical motifs of sacred meal and sacrifice, both of which are important aspects of the Last Supper and Eucharist, and by extension the Mass. He also offers the same erudite treatment of the Real Presence, explaining how the church articulated it with the terminology of "transubstantiation, "accidents" and "substance".[18]

Barron lays out the understanding of the Real Presence, how the Medieval debates shaped the way the Church explains it today. Berengarius of Tours, an eleventh-century French theologian, was condemned by the 1059 Synod for not fully affirming the Real Presence.[19] In large measure, Berengarius can be seen as a harbinger to the later Protestant reformers and the impetus for the Catholic articulation of the Real Presence in the Eucharist. Thus, something good resulted from something bad. So often it is the case that incorrect teaching is the impetus for councils and pronouncements by the Church on what is correct and what is not. The passing of laws in society often works the same way. One needs to delimit the contours of right and wrong, not to inflict punishment so much as to help people know what is best for them, as with matters of morality.

Berengarius' reaction to Christ's presence in the bread and wine of the Eucharist upon consecration was condemned by fourteen different church councils. Berengarius eventually recanted at Rome in 1059. Pope Innocent III is credited as the first to use the term "transubstantiation". He called the Fourth Lateran Council (1215 CE) then a Synod that moved the delineation of the Real Presence along. A little later, Thomas Aquinas would pick up the

18. Barron, *Eucharist*, 95.

19. Barron, *Eucharist*, 86–87.

terms "transubstantiation" and "accident" to crystalize how we today articulate the Eucharist.

Thus Barron lays out a trajectory of Medieval debates that lead to the articulation of the doctrine of the Real Presence by Thomas Aquinas, which was later affirmed at the Council of Trent. This is an example of how Tradition expands on the truth of Scripture, both being necessary sources of authority for the people of God.[20] Fittingly, Barron reminds us that: "Thomas Aquinas said that, though all the sacraments contain the power of Jesus, only the Eucharist contains Jesus himself".[21] Barron states that the Eucharist is the single most important reason one should stay in the church and be faithful to it.[22] Indeed, one could hardly give this sacrament more primacy. Without it, one misses out on the graces of Christ, period. One can therefore say without qualification that it is the single most important thing in the world.

Barron notes that Berengarius is indeed a precursor to the reformers and discusses how modern theologians have attempted to articulate transubstantiation differently in recent years, which ultimately fall short and lacking. Barron excels at distilling doctrines down to their essence for laypeople. For instance, that the terms "substance" and "accidents," can be understood as "reality" and "appearance" respectively is helpful.[23] This is much needed today for laity and non specialists, especially seeing we have became increasingly ignorant of Scripture and of Church teachings in our modern culture. In the preface to his Isaiah commentary, Jerome famously warned that: "Ignorance of Scripture is ignorance of Christ".

Barron also notes that Aquinas maintained that one does not give medicine to a dead person. Thus, not to one in a state of mortal sin, for they are essentially dead in their sin. But he shows that Aquinas contends, as the Church does today, that the Eucharist burns off all venial sin, a point underemphasized today. This

---

20. Vatican II, "Dei Verbum."

21. Barron, *Eucharist*, 73.

22. Barron, *Eucharist*, 74.

23. Barron, *Eucharist*, 95.

coheres with Pope Francis's comments that the Eucharist is medicine for the sick, harmonizing the two perspectives.[24]

Each chapter of Barron's *Eucharist* is devoted to one aspect of the Eucharist: Communion, Sacrifice, and Real Presence. In its long history, the Church emphasized one aspect more than the others. This is only logical. For example, after Vatican II the church emphasized more of the communal meal aspect of the Eucharist at the expense of the sacrificial nature. Thus, the Tridentine Mass arguably stressed this more than the Novus Ordo, but both are important.

24. Francis, *Amoris,* n371; *Evangelii Gaudium,* 47.

Bible Texts

I t is now time to turn our attention to the Bible. What follows is not an exhaustive list, but a review of the main biblical texts pointing to and explaining the Eucharist, first from the Hebrew Scriptures that provide the necessary background to understand the relevant passages in the New Testament. It is crucial to begin with the Hebrew Scriptures because the Catechism reminds us of the necessity to take into account the conditions of the culture in which Yeshua and the Apostles lived. Their modes of feeling and speaking were sometimes quite different from ours as they used prophetic and poetical literary styles to express truth.[1]

Moreover, it is only natural to consider the entire Sacred Scriptures, as what we deem today the Old Testament was for Yeshua himself *the* Bible. Hebrew Bible, Old Testament, and Old Covenant may be used interchangeably. I have opted for the designations Old Covenant for the Hebrew Scriptures and New Covenant for the New Testament for they appropriately capture the themes detailed in this work, though it must be stressed that "Old" is not used in a derogative way in the sense that it is *passé* and has given way to the "New". The ancient world granted more reverence to ancient traditions than we do today. New ideas and concepts were developed by appropriating previous ones rather than out of nothing. How this principle was applied to God is explained in Anderson, *Monotheism*. In fact, the New Covenant is already stated in the Old Covenant.

1. CCC §110.

Genesis 14 &15: Melchizedek and the Covenant with Abram

It is appropriate to begin at the beginning, i.e., in Genesis, the first book of the Bible. Genesis 14 deals with the Canaanite Priest Melchizedek and chapter 15 with God's covenant with Abram who was not yet named Abraham. These chapters are treated together here because Genesis 14 anticipates the Eucharist rendered possible by the covenant in Genesis 15.

The text reads as follows:

> After his return from the defeat of Chedorlaomer and the kings who were with him, the king of Sodom went out to meet him at the Valley of Shaveh (that is, the King's Valley). And King Melchizedek of Salem brought out bread and wine; he was priest of God Most High. He blessed him and said, "Blessed be Abram by God Most High, maker of heaven and earth; and blessed be God Most High, who has delivered your enemies into your hand!"[2]

The somewhat mysterious figure of King Melchizedek of Salem was priest of God Most High. On this basis, the New Covenant declares Yeshua "a priest forever, according to the order of Melchizedek" (Heb 5:6; 6:19; 7:17). Logically, the Church has linked Melchizedek's priesthood with that of Christ.[3] Contrary to priests who presented to God the offerings brought by others, Melchizedek of Salem brought out bread and wine. Consequently, Yeshua offered himself and still offers himself in the elements of the bread and wine.

Note that Melchizedek is the first priest and king mentioned in the Bible, but a priest of God the Most High, that is *El Elyon* in Hebrew. Melchizedek is not an Israelite priest of the Hebrew God because Genesis sets this scene before the birth of Jacob, the ancestor of the tribes of Israel. It is only at the beginning of Exodus, the book that follows Genesis, that we learn with Moses that the real name of the God of Abraham is Yahweh, usually translated in English as

2. Gen 14:17–20.

3. Conner, *Manna*, 229–33.

"The Lord".[4] Therefore, the Bible announces Yeshua right from the beginning, before even the birth of Jacob—Abraham's grandson— and before Moses learns the secret name of the biblical God.

Melchizedek is mentioned again in Ps 110 where the compilers of the Psalter saw a reference to King David, though the Psalm only mentions an anonymous ruler (verse 2). In fact, it is in the New Covenant book of Hebrews that the identity of Melchizedek is unveiled. Having offered himself on the cross, Jesus is then present in the bread and wine of the Eucharist. But there is more. Because Melchizedek is the priest of God the Most High rather than the priest of the Israelite God, Yeshua's sacrifice is not for the benefit of Israelites only but for all of humanity. In their great wisdom, the scribes who penned Genesis 14 understood that if God is God he must be the god of all, even though he is worshipped under differing names by different people groups.[5]

Many Bible readers understand the name Salem, the seat of King Melchizedek, as a reference to Jerusalem, though Jerusalem is *never* mentioned in the Torah—the first five books of the Bible, its most sacred part for the Jews. For this reason, it is more faithful to the sacred text to consider the silence of Jerusalem as another hint of the universality of the biblical message. Melchizedek was the priest of the highest God and Yeshua died in Jerusalem not for Israel only but for all people.

In the next chapter, Genesis 15, Abram is deeply disturbed by his lack of a son of his own to inherit his vast wealth. God asks him to look up at the sky and promises to give him descendants as numerous as the stars and to give him a land as well. But the story continues and Abram replies:

> "O Lord God, how am I to know that I shall possess it?" He said to him, "Bring me a heifer three years old, a female goat three years old, a ram three years old, a turtledove, and a young pigeon." He brought him all these and cut them in two, laying each half over against the other; but he did not cut the birds in two. And when

4. Exod 6:3.

5. Anderson, *El, Yahweh.*

birds of prey came down on the carcasses, Abram drove them away. As the sun was going down, a deep sleep fell upon Abram, and a deep and terrifying darkness descended upon him. . . When the sun had gone down and it was dark, a smoking fire pot and a flaming torch passed between these pieces. On that day the Lord made a covenant with Abram, saying, "To your descendants I give this land, from the river of Egypt to the great river, the river Euphrates, the land of the Kenites, the Kenizzites, the Kadmonites, the Hittites, the Perizzites, the Rephaim, the Amorites, the Canaanites, the Girgashites, and the Jebusites."[6]

There are many intriguing features in this passage, which need deciphering. Those cut up animals and flying torch make little sense to us. These elements feature no barbecue but recall a ratification ceremony during which two rulers would swear faithfulness to one another. Here, however, a major anomaly is introduced in the standard procedure. Instead of having the representatives of the two parties walk between the carcasses of the slaughtered animals essentially stating "may my body be treated as those animals if I break the covenant between you and me," it is a smoking fire pot and a torch that pass between the cut up carcasses.[7] Passing between the pieces of meat underlined the solemnity of the ceremony, warning the swearing parties of the dire consequences of breaking the terms of the pact they are establishing.

Here, the pact, or covenant, is made between God and Abram, though Abram is fast asleep. Or rather, God made him fall into a coma that prevents Abram to walk through the pieces to ratify his participation in the covenant. Does this mean that the covenant is invalid? Not at all. The covenant is duly ratified by the passing of the smoking fire pot and of the flaming torch that stand for the divine party and for Abram too, though he is in no state to accomplish the ritual. Hence, the "deep sleep" that fell upon Abram signifies his inability to perform as a reliable partner in the agreement. Therefore, God acts for both parties in

6. Gen 15:8–12, 17–21.

7. Gen 15:17.

the covenant, something remarkable, as covenants in the ancient world were usually made between kings of equal rank or between a king and his vassal.

That only God passes through the carcasses means that God takes the blame that will occur when the human party, Abraham's descendants, break the terms of the covenant. And it is where Christ intervenes. In essence, God states that regardless of human sins, I will be the one to have my blood spilt. Genesis 15 therefore is already promising that God will die if the people do not hold up their end of the contract. Genesis 14 prefigures the Eucharist and Genesis 15 reveals the coming Atonement of Christ. As is often the case with us feeble humans, the writers may not have understood the implications of their work, but these chapters came to fruition in the Gosples when Jesus implements the New Covenant and the Eucharist during a Passover meal.

Covenant

Further comments are in order on the subject of covenant. Covenants are widely attested in antiquity, usually between kings. In the Bible, God establishes (literally "cuts") a series of covenants: with Noah (Gen 6:18), with Noah and the land animals (Gen 9:11–17), with Abram (Gen 15), Abraham (Gen 17), Moses (Exod 19–24), David (2 Sam 7), Jeremiah (Jer 31:31–34) and with the entire humanity through Christ. The covenant between God and his people may be conceptualized as a contract. It shares similarities with Hittite and Neo-Assyrian treaties in terms of stipulations and penalties. Biblical writers were familiar with these types of agreements.

Logically, the notion of covenant was taken up by Christians. At the Last Supper Jesus explains, "This is my blood of the covenant, which is poured out for many for the forgiveness of sins" (Matt 26:28). The book of Hebrews (9:15) reads, "For this reason Christ is the mediator of a new covenant, that those who are called may receive the promised eternal inheritance, now that he has died as a ransom to set them free from the sins committed under the first covenant." Jesus is described as making the new covenant anticipated by the prophet Jeremiah:

> "The days are coming," declares the Lord, "when I will make a new covenant with the people of Israel and with the people of Judah. It will not be like the covenant I made with their ancestors when I took them by the hand to lead them out of Egypt, because they broke my covenant, though I was a husband to them," declares the Lord. "This is the covenant I will make with the people of Israel after that time," declares the Lord. "I will put my law in their minds and write it on their hearts. I will be their God, and they will be my people. No longer will they teach their neighbor, or say to one another, 'Know the Lord,' because they will all know me, from the least of them to the greatest," declares the Lord. "For I will forgive their wickedness and will remember their sins no more."[8]

This text is quoted in Heb 8:10–12 to underline the fact that Christianity is indebted to Israel's unique notion of a covenant with God and that Yeshua's ministry was anticipated by one of Israel's prophets.

Genesis 22: The Sacrifice of Isaac

Isaac is one of Abraham's sons (Gen 25:2–6), the only one Sarah bore him in their old age. Sarah had given up hope to become a mother and had supplied her own slave girl, Hagar, who bore Abraham's firstborn son, Ishmael. Therefore, when she heard that she would have a son of her own, Sarah laughed, though in fact Isaac's name means "*he* laughed" (Gen 18:12). This long-awaited son was thus very precious and Sarah forced Abraham to send Hagar and Ishmael off to reserve the rank of firstborn for Isaac (Gen 21). As though this was not enough, Abraham was then asked by God to sacrifice Isaac! Abraham obeyed and set off with Isaac, two servants, some fire, a knife and a donkey to carry the wood. As they came close to the dedicated place of sacrifice,

---

8. Jer 31:31–34.

Abraham asked the servants to wait with the donkey and he went ahead with his son who carried the wood, wondering why his father had not taken a lamb to sacrifice. Once there, Abraham built an altar, laid the wood on it, tied Isaac on top of it, hence the name of the scene in Hebrew, the *Akedah*, meaning "Binding". It is only as he rose the knife to slit the throat of his son that an angel stopped him (Gen 22:11).

Having demonstrated that he was ready to give up his son, Abraham found a ram to sacrifice instead of his son. The entire Easter story is there in a nutshell: the father, the son carrying the wooden cross for his own sacrifice, and of course the sacrificial victim who dies for others.

Exodus 12: The Passover Lamb

In Exodus, the next book of the Bible, the ram Abraham sacrifices becomes the lambs sacrificed by each Israelite family on the eve of escaping from Egypt and the harsh Pharaoh who had enslaved them.

Pharaoh repeatedly refused to let Moses' people go, despite the terrible disasters God plagued Egypt with. At first, the Nile water turned into blood, from which developed huge numbers of frogs, gnats, flies, livestock diseases, and boils, followed by hail, thunderstorm, and so many locusts that darkness covered the land for three days, except where the Israelites lived. The final plague is reminiscent of the sacrifice of Isaac as it involved the death of every firstborn son throughout Egypt, including Pharaoh's firstborn son.

To save Israel from this terrible punishment, Moses instructed the Israelites to slaughter a lamb and smear their doorposts with its blood, so that the angel of death would pass over their homes, hence the name of the festival that commemorates the event: the "Pass-over".

For the Jews, Passover celebrates the exit—Exodus—out of Egypt and the liberation from slavery. Christians celebrate Passover at Easter, at the beginning of springtime, as the victory of Jesus over death. Christ is the new Passover lamb about whom

John the Baptist exclaimed, "Behold, the Lamb of God who takes away the sins of the world" (John 1:29). As the Israelites ate the lamb in haste with bread that had no time to raise because they escaped that very night, Christians partake the communal meal every Sunday and even every day because the blood of the Lamb saves us from the slavery of sin. Brant Pitre explains that the meal ratifies the sacrifice in Exodus.[9]

Exodus 16:1–35: Manna in the Wilderness

When the angel of death killed their firstborn sons, the Egyptians urged the Israelites to depart and lent them gold, silver and cloth (Exod 3:22; 11:2). The Israelites thus left Egypt by crossing the sea to begin a new life in the wilderness. Life in the wilderness, however, is harsh as nothing is there to soothe the rocky desolation.

The wilderness is also where Yeshua retreats immediately after his baptism to meditate upon the words that declared him the beloved son of the Father (Matt 3:17; Luke 3:22). For the Israelites, the retreat lasted forty years, during which they were sustained by a daily provision of miraculous food in the form of "a fine flaky substance as fine as frost" that appeared on the ground when the morning dew had lifted (Exod 16:14). It was such a strange phenomenon that the first time they saw it the Israelites asked "What's that," "*man hu?*" in Hebrew, and thus named it "manna".

That miraculous bread from heaven had to be consumed fresh because it became foul overnight, except on the Sabbath. This bread-like substance anticipates another bread that is transformed for our blessing and sustenance too.

Exodus 25:30: Bread of the Presence

While God kept his people alive for forty years in the wilderness, he gave them the blueprints for a mobile sanctuary in which he could be present to journey with his people. This tent housed exquisite

9. Pitre, *Jewish Roots,* 74–76.

paraphernalia, presumably made with some of the gold borrowed from the Egyptians. The tent housed a wooden table covered with gold complete with rings and poles to transport it. On this table, a special kind of bread was displayed on golden plates and dishes. This *leḥem panim,* literally "bread of faces" is usually translated as "bread of the presence" or "show bread" as the text specifies that it must be "on the table before me always" (Exod 25:30).

The writers seem to have conceived this bread after the long conical loaves piled up on top of other offerings in Egyptian altar scenes. For us, this bread is the model for the consecrated bread stored besides every consecrated altar throughout the world rather than at a single temple because God is always on the move.

Numbers 11:31–35: Quails

Tasting like "wafers made with honey" (Exod 16:31), the manna was nevertheless a monotonous menu and the magic soon wore off. The Israelites began craving for the Nile perch, the fresh onions, the cucumbers, melons, leeks and garlic they ate in Egypt (Num 11:5). Protests and weeping were heard throughout the camp. Moses was displeased and God became angry at such ingratitude. Moses was ready to give up and let the people go back to Egypt. Only a major show of force could overturn the crisis. It took the form of an enormous flight of quails that dropped on the camp. The Israelites feasted on the fat birds for a day, two days, five days, and for a whole month until it came out of their nostrils and they were utterly sick of it (Num 11:19).

This is a crucial lesson for anyone insisting on quantity while failing to understand the value of a tiny wafer received at Holy Communion.

Joshua 2: Rahab's Red Thread

The Exodus eventually came to an end and Israel was ready to enter the Promised Land. The Exodus lasted forty years because the people first refused to enter earlier when they heard the report of the twelve scouts Moses had sent to spy the land and prepare the conquest (Num 14:1–4). Taking no chance, Moses sent again only two spies to reconnoiter the land of Jericho.

Instead of touring the land, the spies focused on the city itself. After forty years of wilderness, civilization's appeals were irresistible. They stopped at the inn by the city gate where they enjoyed the pleasures available in such places before retiring to the roof top for a good sleep. The brothel-keeper, however, soon realized whom her two guests were when guards came to seize them. A quick thinker, she pretended that they had already left. While a party was sent to pursue them towards the Jordan River, Rahab hurried to the roof and woke the spies up to strike a deal they were in no position to refuse: Your life against mine. If I save your life, swear that you will save mine. The spies duly swore and before fleeing they indicated the crimson cord with which they were let down outside the city walls (recall Paul at Damascus in Acts 9:25) as the sign to identify Rahab's house when the Israelites would storm the city (Josh 2:18–20).

As promised, the spies were sent to rescue Rahab when Jericho fell and the entire population was slaughtered. Rahab was not alone. Her entire family as well as everyone else who took refuge behind her door was saved (Josh 6:22–25).

In recognition for her generosity, Matthew (1:5) added Rahab in the list of Yeshua's ancestors, while James (2:25) cites her as the model for a living faith that produces good works. The Book of Hebrews (11:31) lists Rahab along the heroes of the faith besides Abraham and Moses.

Therefore, Rahab's crimson cord literally is the red thread that connects the Exodus of the Hebrews out of slavery to the sacrifice of Yeshua who saves those who believe in the saving power of his blood.

Elijah and Elisha

The great prophets of Israel, Elijah and his successor Elisha, also foreshadow the future coming of the Eucharist. After being afraid for his life because of threats by Jezebel, even to the point of desiring to die, Elijah is comforted by an angel near Beersheba and given the sustenance of life, namely bread (1 Kgs 19:6). Even more significant for how Yeshua later comes to us, are the miracles of food multiplication God performs via his messengers: flour, oil, bread, and fresh ears of grain (1 Kgs 17; 2 Kgs 4:1–7, 41–44). Jesus himself multiplies bread (John 6). All of these anticipate the Eucharist.

Jeremiah 31:31–34: A New Covenant

We now jump over a good dozen of biblical books to the Prophet Jeremiah. Whereas Rahab saw the arrival of the Hebrews in the Promised Land, Jeremiah experienced the final decade of the Kingdom of Judah. As a courtier employed by the royal administration, Jeremiah got into trouble during the initial siege of Jerusalem by the Neo-Babylonian army in 599–597 BCE. As he had advised surrender because he doubted that God would save the city, Jeremiah was considered a traitor and arrested (Jer 37:16).

A political realist, Jeremiah perceived that his world had come to an end and that the kingdoms of Israel and Judah were irremediably absorbed into vast Empires against which all resistance was suicidal. Hence, he envisioned a new way to serve God, a New Covenant that would make it possible to live one's faith anywhere, irrespective of political vagueries, in Babylon as much as in Egypt:

> The days are surely coming, says the Lord, when I will make a new covenant with the house of Israel and the house of Judah. It will not be like the covenant that I made with their ancestors when I took them by the hand to bring them out of the land of Egypt—a covenant that they broke, though I was their husband, says the Lord. But this is the covenant that I will make with the house

of Israel after those days, says the Lord: I will put my law within them, and I will write it on their hearts; and I will be their God, and they shall be my people. No longer shall they teach one another, or say to each other, "Know the Lord," for they shall all know me, from the least of them to the greatest, says the Lord; for I will forgive their iniquity, and remember their sin no more.[10]

Jeremiah realized that the kingdom of Judah was about to fall as the kingdom of Israel had fallen a century-and-a-half earlier. Jerusalem had become an overripe fruit that God was not going to rescue. Instead of relying on a king to enforce law and order, the New Covenant would involve people who had the law inscribed in their heart. But before we leave the Old Covenant to enter the New Covenant, the strangest of all prophetic books offers a most vivid prefiguration of Christ.

The Sign of Jonah

On the night the Israelites fled Egypt, they passed through the sea that was opened before them. In the ancient world, the Sea was a mighty deity that signified chaos (Job 26:12; Ps 89:10); chaos as a sea monster.[11] After a long and terrifying fight, a young god managed to split opened the chaotic Sea to create a space for life. Following the same pattern, the Israelites slaves cross the Sea to begin a new life as much as Christians receive the saving sacrament of Baptism.

Water imagery is profound. Water is both essential to life and a threat, in particular for sailors when they are caught in a storm. In four short chapters, the story of Jonah combines the threatening and life-giving aspects of the watery world.

At first, Jonah refuses to go to Nineveh, the great city of the Assyrians, to warn it that the wickedness of its inhabitants has reached God. Simple as it sounds, that mission is like being sent to a dictator's palace to criticize his policies. No wonder Jonah

10. Jer 31:31–34.

11. Anderson, *Extolling Yeshua*, 14–19.

boards a boat to escape to the other side of the world. But can anyone be out of reach of the God of heaven who made the sea and the dry land (Jonah 1:9)?

God hurled a mighty wind upon the sea and the sailors were terrified. Meanwhile, Jonah was fast asleep in the hull. The captain had to wake him up, asking him to implore his own god to calm the storm. Having cast lots, the sailors found out that Jonah was the cause of the storm and that he was fleeing from his God. At Jonah's request, they threw Jonah overboard. The sea stilled instantly and the sailors were saved.

To underline the prophetic character of Jesus' ministry, the Gospel of Mark has Yeshua fast asleep on the cushion at the stern of the boat when it is caught in a storm on the Sea of Galilee (Mark 4:38). The frightened disciples have to wake him before he rebukes the gale and saves them.

Jonah too was saved when a great fish swallowed him only to vomit him three days later on a beach in the direction of Nineveh. While in the belly of the fish, Jonah got the impression that he was in the belly of Sheol, the Hebrew term for the underworld (Jonah 2:2). The passage of a prophet in the underworld was not lost on the Christians who applied it to the days between the crucifixion and the resurrection on Easter morning. Jonah became a sign, the only sign Yeshua agrees to give to those who came to test him (Matt 16:4). Luke 11:32 adds that the people of Nineveh (destroyed in 612 BCE) would rise up at the Last Judgement to condemn those who reject Yeshua.

The sign of Jonah is relevant to the Eucharist, as the scene of the storm is taken over in the gospels with Yeshua asleep in the boat to underline his power over the elements and the lack of faith of his disciples (Matt 8:23–27, Mark 4:35–41, and Luke 8:22–25). Let us now turn our attention to the New Covenant.

Luke 22: The Institution of the Eucharist

Exodus 12 considered above is the basis for understanding Yeshua as the Passover lamb. As he shared his Last Supper with his disciples, Yeshua commanded them to celebrate the Eucharist in perpetuity:

> When the hour came, he took his place at the table, and the apostles with him. He said to them, "I have eagerly desired to eat this Passover with you before I suffer; for I tell you, I will not eat it until it is fulfilled in the kingdom of God." Then he took a cup, and after giving thanks he said, "Take this and divide it among yourselves; for I tell you that from now on I will not drink of the fruit of the vine until the kingdom of God comes." Then he took a loaf of bread, and when he had given thanks, he broke it and gave it to them, saying, "This is my body, which is given for you. Do this in remembrance of me." And he did the same with the cup after supper, saying, "This cup that is poured out for you is the new covenant in my blood."[12]

There is no ambiguity in Yeshua's words. He declares "this is my body." He does not say "this is a symbol" but "this is my body". The concluding lines of this important text recalls Jeremiah's announcement of a new covenant and appropriates it for Yeshua, claiming that it comes to fruition through his sacrifice. Breaking bread and partaking of a cup of wine are part of the Passover meal Jews celebrate to remember the last night of the Hebrews in Egypt and their escape.

To an ancient Semitic audience "do this in remembrance of me" would mean something much deeper than mere memories of a past event. In biblical Hebrew, "to remember" (*zakar*) can mean "to recall, to reenact" and even "to reproduce" since the name *zakar* designates the male, i.e., the father who transmits the family heritage from one generation to the next. To share the broken loaf and partake the cup that reenact Yeshua's last Passover meal with his disciples is to make him present as he says he would be after having completed his sacrifice.

Jews today relive the night the Hebrews ran away from Egypt by reading the relevant passage in Exodus and sharing a symbolic meal with bits of actual foods such as unleavened bread, a bone,

---

12. Luke 22:14–20. Compare Matt 26:26–29; Mark 14:22–25.

and bitter herbs.[13] Christians are called to experience, not merely remember, the past event of Yeshua's sacrifice on the cross.

Sacrifice is but the first step to a meal. The lamb is sacrificed in order to be eaten. Exodus 12:10 insists that the lamb must be eaten completely on that night: "let none of it remain until morning!" Any remains must be burned right away. To avoid any waste, verse 4 advises households too small for a whole lamb to "join its closest neighbor".

Finally, "do this in remembrance of me!" is a command, not something optional. As much as taking food on a daily basis is basic to a healthy life, accomplishing the order to partake in the Last Supper is basic to spiritual health.

The Church maintains that the Last Supper was a Passover meal:

> By celebrating the Last Supper with his apostles in the course of the Passover meal, Jesus gave the Jewish Passover its definitive meaning. Jesus' passing over to his father by his death and Resurrection, the new Passover, is anticipated in the Supper and celebrated in the Eucharist, which fulfills the Jewish Passover and anticipates the final Passover of the Church in the glory of the kingdom.[14]

The Gospels present small variations regarding the time of Yeshua's exact moment of death because they put the emphasis on different parts of the Passover meal, but the four Gospels agree that Yeshua's sacrifice occurred during the great Passover festival in Jerusalem and that Passover is the adequate framework to understand the Easter story.[15]

The Catechism of the Catholic Church explains: "By celebrating the Last Supper with his apostles in the course of the Passover mean, Jesus gave the Jewish Passover it definitive meaning".[16] Thus, the teaching authority of the church understands it as a Passover meal. Jesus was portrayed as the Passover lamb, and the

---

13. Klawans, "Seder," 24–47.

14. CCC §1340.

15. Sandnes, "Last Meal," 275–312.

16. CCC §1340.

meal instituted something new, the celebration of the New Covenant in the Eucharist until Christ comes again.

Though the Synoptics Gospels and John have some differences in terms of details regarding the Passover week in Jerusalem when Yeshua was crucified, it is clear that the Passover festival is the key to explain the work of Christ, his sacrifice, and the meal that ratifies it—the Eucharist. Yeshua is portrayed as the Passover lamb. As noted above, when he sees Yeshua who comes to him to be baptized, John the Baptist explains: "Behold the lamb of God who takes away the sins of the world" (John 1:29).

Luke 24:13–25: Seeing Yeshua in the Breaking of Bread

The death of Yeshua left his disciples in a state of confusion. It took several encounters with the risen Christ before they could make sense of what they had experienced during the years they had spent with him. One such encounter takes place on the road to Emmaus where he joins two of his disciples who inform him that some women claim that he was alive.

Though Jesus explains to them that this is exactly what the prophets had long foretold, it is only as he takes bread and blesses it that they recognized him (Luke 24:13–25). It is the breaking of bread that opens their eyes and allows the disciples to recognize the risen Yeshua. The breaking of bread is an obvious reference to the Eucharist as it reenacts the last supper Yeshua shared with his disciples.

John 2:1–11: Wine at Cana

Contrary to the other gospels, John's does not wait for the end of Yeshua's career to underline the sacramental power of the bread and wine of the last supper. The very first miracle Yeshua performs is changing water into wine at a wedding in Cana, an episode unique to John.

The text states that Yeshua's mother was present. It is the first mention of Mary because John, like Mark, does not narrate the Christmas story. Instead of Yeshua's birth, John 2 begins with his coming of age.

Though verse 2 adds that the disciples were there too, they are mere spectators, contrary to Mary who plays a pivotal role as the new Ark and new Eve. She helps reverse the sin of Adam and Eve in a sacred parallelism with her son. Like the Ark of the Covenant, she carried the Word of God inside her for a time. Recalling David who leaps before the Ark (2 Sam 16:15–16), John leaped in Elizabeth's womb before Yeshua (Luke 1:41–42). It is at the prompting of his mother that Yeshua performs his first miracle (John 2:3). In this way, she prompts her son to become a man and accepts that he will go away from her. With the reproachful tone of his answer "Woman, what concern is that to you and to me?" Yeshua answers Mary's prompting with an indication that implies an immediate change in their relation. To Yeshua, Mary is not mother anymore, but woman. The greatest miracle at Cana is not so much the water turned into first class wine, but the self-sacrificial example of a mother who willingly sends off her son, something every mother experiences as painful, in a sense a second birthing.

John 6: Bread Multiplied

The four gospels report the scene of Yeshua's feeding a multitude by multiplying a few loaves of bread (Matt 14:13–21; Mark 6:32–44; Luke 9:10b–17; John 6:1–15). The occasion and the numbers involved differ, but the scenes are a foreshadowing of how Christ feeds us with his bread. In the Gospel of John, he explicitly contends that he is "bread of life come down from heaven" (John 6:51).

John 6 is by all means the most important text for explaining the Eucharist as it can be read as the outline of the Mass, with the liturgy of the Word at the beginning, followed by a discourse on eating his flesh, the liturgy of the Eucharist. In this chapter, we find one of the seven "I am" statements of Yeshua that appear only in the Gospel of John: "I am the bread of life" (John 6:35). With these "I am" statements, Jesus evokes his divinity by ascribing to himself the somewhat cryptic divine name "I am who I am" (Exod 3:14).

Two chapters on, Yeshua adds "before Abraham was, I am" (John 8:58), which the Jews understand as outright blasphemy and try to stone him. As his time was yet to come, Yeshua leaves the temple, which underlines that the bread of life will not be dispensed by temple priests anymore. Connecting divinity with bread, the I-am statement marks the ability of the bread of life to be ever present before and after Abraham.

Jesus' teaching in John 6 shatters the idea that the Eucharist is merely a symbol and comes from the founder of the faith and the Bible itself. In saying "I am the bread of life," Jesus claims that he himself is the substance of life. Three times Jesus insists that his flesh must be eaten, or even "gnawed or chewed" as the Greek verb *trosan* suggests (John 6:53–56). More is involved than simply ingesting food to satiate hunger temporarily. This was too much for some disciples to stomach and many "turned back and no longer went about with him" (John 6:66). Yeshua simply lets them depart from him. He does not say, "Wait, I mean it only symbolically!"

Whatever arguments are advanced to read the chewing of Yesha's flesh in a symbolic sense, the classic Catholic response is logical and sound. "Unless you eat the flesh of the Son of Man and drink his blood, you have no life in you." This means what it means: you have life in you when you partake of the mystery of the Eucharist.

Chewing a man's flesh and drinking is blood is cannibalism, an accusation leveled at Christians, as Justin Martyr reports in his *First Apology*. Chewing a god's flesh and drinking a god's blood is an entirely different matter. For an ancient audience, it evoked certain rituals such as those associated with the cult of Dionysos, a god who died and rose again following the seasons.

The cult of Dionysus was ubiquitous in antiquity. People went into the god's temple and feasted on meat dedicated to the god. It is quite possible that John used imagery from the cult of Dionysos to convey the Eucharistic mysteries, which in no way validates a mere symbolic understanding of the bread of life as

Yeshua's body. On the contrary, it underlines his divinity and the need to give up rational explanation.

The Eucharist involves partaking the life substance of Christ as the Son of Man, a divine title. The Eucharist is no ordinary meal. It is a sacrificial meal. What is consumed is the flesh and blood of the lamb of God who came down from heaven.

John 19:34: Yeshua's Piercing

The Gospel of John mentions a unique detail during the crucifixion (John 19:34). As the Sabbath was approaching, the soldiers in charge of the execution were asked to speed up the death of the three condemned by breaking their legs. Noting that Yeshua had already expired, one of the soldiers pierced his side with a spear, "and at once blood and water came out" (John 19:34). This makes little sense except as a reference to the Eucharist and Baptism as Saint John Chrysostom explains. The water and blood that flow from Yeshua' side at Golgotha symbolize the two most important sacraments of the Church, Baptism, and Holy Communion.

Baptism brings one into the communion of faith, the body of Christ; Communion sustains one on the road of life and dispenses God's grace from the cross to us as often as we desire to partake of it.

At the Cross, these two sacraments are brought together: Baptist as the sacrament of initiation; the Eucharist as the food to sustain us on our life journey and for our transition to the next life.

First Corinthians 10:16–17: One in the Eucharist

Leaving the gospels, we turn to Paul who wrote that "the cup of blessing that we bless, is it not a sharing in the blood of Christ? The bread that we break, is it not a sharing in the body of Christ? Because there is one bread, we who are many are one body, for we all partake of the one bread" (1 Cor 1:16–17).

In agreement with John, Paul is clear that as we partake of the Eucharist, we are partaking in the body of Christ. Additionally, we become one body in Christ. The Eucharist binds Christians into one body, the body of Christ, made up of differing parts. Emphasizing the corporate body of Christ was a particular favorite for Paul, the Apostle to the Gentiles.

First Corinthians 11:23–29: Discerning the Body

The institution of the Last Supper in 1 Corinthians 11:23–29 coheres with the gospels and the teaching of the Church.[17] Paul did not take the Eucharist as a mere symbol, for he explains that it is dangerous to partake of it unworthily:

> Whoever, therefore, eats the bread or drinks the cup of the Lord in an unworthy manner will be answerable for the body and blood of the Lord. Examine yourselves, and only then eat of the bread and drink of the cup. For all who eat and drink without discerning the body, eat and drink judgment against themselves. For this reason many of you are weak and ill, and some have died.[18]

A scary text! The apostle to the Gentiles could hardly have penned these words had he not understood the Real Presence of Christ in the Eucharist! This is where we get the understanding that one should not come to communion aware of mortal sin they have committed, least they hurt themselves, for it is harmful. For this reason the Church requires recourse to the Sacrament of Reconciliation to be forgiven of moral sins before taking Communion, ensuring one is not harmed. It is not a punishment.

Now, what does the phrase: "discerning the body" mean? Is it a reference to all members of the body of Christ or to Yeshua's body we partake in the Mass, namely the Real Presence of Christ in the Eucharist? Protestants opt for the corporate body of Christ, but the context is clearly in favor of the body of Jesus himself. The

17. CCC §1457.

18. 1 Cor 11:27–29.

same Greek term "*soma*" ("body") is used in the previous verses in reference to Yeshua: "this is my body" (verse 24) and the "body and blood of the Lord" (verse 27). Paul uses the Greek term *ekklesia* in verses 16, 18, and 22 for the Church. In the context of the institution of the Last Supper here, the "body *and blood* of the Lord" can only refer to the bread and wine of the Eucharist when the Church partakes of the body and blood of the Lord. Never is the Church imagined as partaking of its own body. This has always been the teaching of the Church. Even Protestant reformer Martin Luther understood the body in this text to be a reference to the Real Presence, not to the members of the Church.[19]

Finally, the Greek verb "to discern" (*diakrino*) is never used in the New Covenant in relation to the Church. *Diakrino* always carries a negative connotation, an injunction not to do something. Thus, "discerning the body" is a call to be aware that the bread is the body of Yeshua, i.e., to take the Real Presence of Christ in the Eucharist very seriously. This is the plain meaning of the institution of the Last Supper. It is always possible to explain away the plain meaning of a text one dislikes, but if a text can be interpreted to mean the opposite of its plain meaning, there is no point to appeal to the authority of Scripture. Sadly, Protestant readings of "discerning the body" as a reference to the Church simply reject the plain meaning of 1 Corinthians 11.

Paul's warning to discern Yeshua's body in 1 Corinthians 11:23–29 is the reason why the Church contends that one should not come to the Eucharist in the awareness of having committed a mortal sin because this would be "judgement against themselves" as Paul warns (1 Cor 11:29). In this case, one may ask whether the Eucharist is medicine, poison, or both?

Medicine is good to fight diseases, but it must be taken cautiously, according to a medical prescription that determines the recommended daily intake to obtain the desired result. Taking too little has minimal effect. Taking too much will cause harm. Hence, the best medicine can turn out to be useless or poisonous,

---

19. Luther, *Heavenly Prophets*, II.

depending on how it is taken. Now, what does this mean in regard to the Eucharist?

Seldom participation in the Mass is like taking too little medicine. In fact, what Paul refers to as eating the bread and drinking the cup "in an unworthy manner is not a matter of quantity but a matter of misuse of the medicine of the "body and blood of the Lord". Exactly in the same way as the Ten Commandments forbid using the name of the Lord in vain or making a wrongful use of it (Deut 5:11), Paul warns that the Eucharist is no light matter.

Pope Francis's sentiment on the Eucharist is helpful and what I go by: it is medicine for the sick, not a weapon. He has never denied anyone communion. This coheres with his sentiment that the Church is a field hospital for the sick. His apostolic exhortation *Amoris Laetitia* expresses the desire to open up communion to more people. I think this wise in light of what it is and because coming to Christ in the Eucharist heals and transforms people. But it is a sticky issue and a dividing line between conservative and liberal Catholics.

In conclusion, the Eucharist is medicine for the sick, as Pope Francis explains. According to the words of Jesus: "Those who are well have no need of a physician, but those who are sick; I have come to call not the righteous but sinners" (Mark 2:17; see Matt 9:12–13; Luke 5:31). The Eucharist is the healing balm and medicine we need for our spiritual ills. For the most part, Catholic liberals will contend it is medicine for the sick, as does Pope Francis. He is portrayed saying such in recent movie, the 2019 *The Two Popes*. His *Amoris Laetitia* suggests the Church ought to welcome divorcees to the Eucharist to take into account the complexity of family situations in the present society. The Pope desires to let more people access this spiritual medicine. It is hard to believe that those coming to Christ in the Eucharist would be hurt by it, as long as they do not so in a brazen, haughty, and irreverent manner.

Conversely, conservatives want its access to remain more circumscribed. This view presupposes that it can be dangerous, as 1 Corinthians suggests. Thus, there is a real tension here. No doubt this text argues in favor of the seriousness of partaking of the Eucharist according to the Apostle Paul. So, both positions are theologically sound. Catholic liberals and conservatives are correct in spite of taking opposite positions. Hard as this is to square with common logic, when dealing with the divine it makes perfect sense. Both positions are correct in the same way as Rabbinic Judaism justaposes differing and opposing interpretations of texts to illuminate deep truths.

The analogy of medicine is most appropriate. Just like good medicine, the consecrated bread and wine can heal, or hurt when not taken correctly as prescribed. Opening up access to the Eucharist to a degree is perhaps a solution, the issue being precisely how much it should be opened so more can partake of its benefits. This is best left for theologians of the Church to flesh out, but it is a vitally important topic no doubt, for the healing balm of Christ can also work against one if not taken properly. This is no trivial debate, but both liberals and conservatives agree that Christ is present in the Eucharist.

Revelation 5: The Crucified Lamb of God

It is appropriate to conclude our survey of New Covenant by pointing to the Eucharist in the final book of the New Testament, Revelation, as the testimony to the Passover lamb continues right until the end of the Bible. In Revelation 5, John views a scroll in the hand of someone sitting on *the* throne. The scroll in question has writing on both sides and it is sealed with seven seals. Then John hears a mighty sound asking in a loud voice:

> "Who is worthy to break the seals and open the scroll?"
> But no one in heaven or on earth or under the earth could open the scroll or even look inside it. I wept and wept because no one was found who was worthy to open the scroll or look inside.[20]

Only one was found worthy of the sacred task of taking the scroll from the hand of the One who sat on the throne, to break the seven

20. Rev 5:1–4.

seals and open it. He is the Lamb who is praised by thousands of angels. The Lamb bore the marks of having been sacrificed. By the blood of his sacrifice he obtained from God "persons from every tribe and language and people and nation" (Rev 5:9).

This passage envisions a glorious liturgy that contains all the important elements of the Mass: Christ as the slain lamb, the praise and worship of the lamb.

Further on, we learn of the marriage supper of the lamb, a sacred meal after the wedding, one we are invited to: "Blessed are those who are invited to the marriage supper of the Lamb. And he said to me, "These are the true words of God" (Rev 19:9).

The wedding feast can also be thought of as the ratification of the sacrifice noted in this work as necessary, just as the Passover sacrifice was ratified in Exodus. The sacrifice of Christ is ratified every time we eat the Eucharistic sacrifice. The wedding feast is the heavenly version of the feast we celebrate at the Eucharist. The nuptial aspect and character of Christ's work is another important one, but it exceeds the purview of this short primer.

Revelation points to the sacramental meal of the Lamb and explicitly portrays Yeshua as the Lamb sacrificed for the sins of the world (Rev 13:8) making use of the important motif examined above from Exodus 12. Revelation unmistakably points to Christ as the Passover lamb, atonement thorough him and a meal, thus the Eucharist. It is astonishing how this one book has it all. Just as before the Exodus the Hebrews had a communal meal ratifying the Passover sacrifice, so Christ's new exodus has the communal meal of the Eucharist continually ratifying Christ's sacrifice. It is not a new sacrifice, but his one-for-all sacrifice at Calvary.

That those who are blessed are those who are invited to the marriage supper of the Lamb does not exclude anyone because Yeshua died for the sins of the world and all are invited to the wedding Supper. Many do not respond to the invitation, but if you are reading this, know that you are invited to the Supper and God wants you to come.

To conclude this chapter, the biblical material could hardly be clearer. Our biblical itinerary began in Genesis right through

to Jonah and to the Institution narratives in the Synoptic Gospels (Matt 26:26–29; Mark 14:22–25; Luke 22:14–20). Though
presented from a different angle in John 6, Paul's institution of
the Eucharist for the Corinthians is no different. Closing with
the heavenly vision of the glorious lamb in Revelation, the Bible
maps out the ways God is present to us. For the New Covenant,
whenever and wherever a consecrated priest pronounces the liturgical words "this is my body," God offers us spiritual medicine
as the mystical body of Christ when we partake in the body and
blood of Christ (1 Cor 10:16–17). These are no mere words. They
have the power to heal and make us grow when we take the Eucharist worthily and regularly. Having run the biblical track from
Genesis to Revelation, we now focus on a few biblical clues il-
luminating the Eucharist before considering the writings of some
early Christian theologians in the final chapter.

Bethlehem and Super-Substantial Bread

Bethlehem, Yeshua's Birthplace

According to the Christmas story in the Gospel of Luke, Yeshua's birth in Bethlehem was somewhat accidental. It was because they obeyed an edict of the Roman Emperor that his parents had to travel there from Nazareth in order to be officially registered in the census. The Gospel of Matthew ignores the Roman Emperor and is more explicit on the reasons why Yeshua was born at Bethlehem. It was because Joseph was from the royal house of David that Yeshua was born in Bethlehem.

In Hebrew, Bethlehem literally translates house (*beth*) of bread (*leḥem*). A third reason for Yeshua's birth there is an ancient prophecy that the Shepherd and Ruler of Israel would come from Bethlehem (Mic 5:1–4a).

In Hebrew, *Beth* can also mean "dynasty" and "temple" in addition to an ordinary house. Therefore, Bethlehem can equally be rendered as "Temple of Bread." As women baked the bread for their family at home, it is unlikely that the name derives from a baking industry that would have been significant enough to name Bethlehem as such. Another unlikely hypothesis is that the name derives from a god *leḥem* that would have been worshipped there. Though it is true that other places were named after a local divinity, the problem with Bethlehem is that no such god is attested anywhere in antiquity, despite the many other Canaanite divinities that archaeologists have retrieved. Therefore, the actual origins of the name of Yeshua's birthplace remains unknown. We are thus free to suggest a theological interpretation, without claiming that it explains the actual etymology of Bethlehem.

Since Yeshua explains that he is the bread of life (John 6:35, 48, 51) and that the Gospels and Paul agree that his Real Presence appears in the Eucharist celebrated daily and venerated at Adoration, perhaps it is by God's providential design that the bread of life, Yeshua, was born in a place that can be literally translated as "Temple of Bread" or "House of Bread." Yeshua thus came from the house of bread and is the very bread of life himself. He is portrayed as the new temple in John 2:20–21 and he is the temple of bread in a very literal way.

We can marvel at God's providential design that set the birth of the future Messiah at the Temple of Bread to announce the future Eucharist. For the fulfillment of prophecy for the coming of the Messiah (Mic 5:2) also hinted at what he would later institute and how his grace would be extended to us. From the Temple of Bread, the bread of life is given to sustain us throughout this life. Another fascinating hint is found in the Lord's Prayer.

Super-Substantial Bread

During his ministry in Palestine, Yeshua taught his disciples how to prayer. He taught them what has come to be known as the Lord's Prayer or Our Father. The prayer is recorded in two of the Synoptic Gospels, Matthew and Luke. In both versions, the same Greek term is used, which likely stands as a clue foreshadowing the coming Eucharist. This prayer that unites all Christians of every confession includes a reference to bread: "Give us this bread our daily bread" (Matt 6:11; Luke 11:3).

The term translated as "daily" is *epousion*, a Greek term used nowhere else in Scripture. Translators have long noted the difficulty in translating this term as "daily" fails to express all the meanings of *epousion*. Besides a day-by-day provision of bread or a provision of bread for the coming day, *epousion* also conveys bread "necessary for existence." Saint Jerome went further and opted for "super-substantial bread," in Matthew's gospel. Therefore, the daily bread we pray for is more than simply the daily ration we need to survive, it is "extraordinary and supernatural" bread to cover the needs of a healthy spiritual life.

The simple translation of "daily" in English obscures this issue, but "daily" has reigned supreme for centuries. Jerome's lead has not been followed, though the notion of a super-substantial bread certainly points to the bread we partake in at the Eucharist.

Viewing this bread as more than mere bread reflects what we have found so far by considering the other passages of the Bible. Alluding to the Eucharist in the prayer he taught us, Yeshua asks us to implore him for our spiritual food and subsistence for the journey of life.

That Yeshua was born in Bethlehem and that he teaches us to pray for supernatural bread hint at the coming Eucharist he institutes at the Last Supper. God in his brilliance and hiddenness points to the way he will relate to his people, through his Blessed Sacrament.

The Witness of the
Church Fathers

F ollowing the teachings of the Scriptures, the early church gathered to celebrate the Eucharist (Acts 2:42). Documents written right after the texts of the New Covenant such as the second-century CE *Didache* took the Real Presence of Christ in the Eucharist for granted. Hence, instead of discussing it, it warned to "let no one eat or drink of your Eucharist, unless they have been baptized into the name of the Lord; for concerning this also the Lord has said, 'Give not that which is holy to the dogs.'"

As is still the case in the Church today, the *Didache* reserved the celebration of the Eucharist for the baptized members of the Christian community, precisely because the bread and wine were no mere remembrance but were holy and thus required to be treated with the reverence reserved for sanctity.

This "confirms what the Church had always thought, namely, that the Real Presence was the uniform belief of ancient Christianity".[1] The "early Church Fathers uniformly affirmed the Real Presence of Christ's body and blood".[2] P. Madrid, citing St. Ignatius of Antioch's *Letter to the Smyrnaeans* 6:2–7:1, writes regarding the Eucharist:

> This was the faith of the earliest Christians, as testified to by leading figures of the young church, such as Saint

1. Howell, *Eucharist*, 54.
2. Howell, *Eucharist*, 53; see also Ray, *Tiber*, 215–54.

Ignatius of Antioch, who would be martyred around 107. He was a disciple of John the apostle and learned the doctrine of the Eucharist directly from him, an eyewitness to the Last Supper. "Take note," he said, "of those who hold heterodox opinions on the grace of Jesus Christ which has come to us, and see how contrary their opinions are to the mind of God. [. . .] They abstain from the Eucharist and from prayer because they do not confess that the Eucharist is the flesh of our savior Jesus Christ, flesh which suffered for our sins and which that Father, in his goodness, raised up again. They who deny the gift of God are perishing in their disputes."[3]

Being able to rely on a source that dates prior to 107 CE is remarkably early from a historian's point of view. The disciples of Yeshua had only recently passed away. It is thought that the apostle John had only died seven years earlier. According to St. Irenaeus of Lyons, Polycarp knew the disciple John and Ignatius knew Polycarp as well as John. It is highly unlikely that John would have understood the Eucharist differently than did Ignatius. John was with Yeshua and knew what he taught. As discussed above in relation to John 6, John believed in the Real Presence. Only two generations had passed between Yeshua's death and Ignatius' life, so it is reasonable to consider that information was passed on with minimal change.

Ignatius was a well-know and venerated bishop in Asia Minor (modern-day Turkey). This is one reason his letter was respected and preserved. Thus, belief in the Real Presence goes back to John and was passed on correctly to Ignatius via John and Polycarp. The evidence suggests Polycarp also conversed with a few of the other disciples who were with Yeshua as well.[4] This too suggests that Yeshua's disciples believed in the real presence of Christ in the Eucharist.

For early Christians like Ignatius of Antioch who knew John the Apostle, the Eucharist they celebrated was not merely a symbol of Jesus, nor a mere memorial meal. It was the Real Presence of Christ and thus the same Eucharist Catholics and Orthodox

3. Madrid, *Ten Answers*, 57–58.
4. Heschmeyer, *Early Church*, 25–32.

celebrate today. It is the body and blood of Christ that allows us to have life in us (John 6) and to be assured of resurrection on the last day at the end of time (John 6). For the first 1,500 years of its history, the Church took the Real Presence of Christ in the Eucharist for granted. The debate over it arose only in the last 500 years, which in itself is an argument in favor of the Real Presence, all the more so as Protestants differ between themselves over the alternative. It is very unfortunate that the theological fights of the sixteenth century led Protestants to deny the Real Presence. These theological divisions were most often spurred by political dissensions, but the end result was negative for all concerned. Whatever Ignatius meant in his letter quoted above, the disputes caused much suffering following the Protestant Reformation. One prays for reunification. The similarity in practice and doctrine between the Catholic and Orthodox Churches is one reason full communion between the two is likely to occur before it occurs with the Protestants.

Justin Martyr

Justin Martyr is one of our earliest Christian writers. Around 150 CE, he described in his *First Apology* what the early Church did when it gathered. It is a remarkable text for it essentially provides the same rubric of the Mass that is still in effect today. The document is a blueprint for the Mass of the early Church. The liturgy of the Word is followed by a liturgy of the Eucharist, just as it does at our Mass today and all the Masses since the time of Martyr until and our day. Regarding the Eucharist, he wrote:

> And this food is called among us "Eucharist," of which no one is allowed to partake but the one who believes that the things which we teach are true, and who has been washed with the washing that is for the remission of sins and unto a second birth, and who is so living as Christ has enjoined. For not as common bread and common drink do we receive these, but in like manner as Jesus Christ our Savior, having been made flesh by the word of God, had both flesh and blood for our

salvation, so likewise have we been taught that the food which is blessed by the word of prayer transmitted from him, and by which our blood and flesh by assimilation and nourished, is the flesh and blood of that Jesus who was made flesh.[5]

Cleary this early Church father believed in the Real Presence! For this reason, Justin insists that one must be cleansed from sins to eat of it, just as the Church today requires the Sacrament of Reconciliation if one is aware of grave sins before approaching the Eucharist. The continuity between the early Church and today's Catholic teaching is remarkable.[6] This excerpt is also reminiscent of Paul's words to the Corinthians discussed above, i.e., that no one should partake of the Eucharist unworthily.

Saint Cyril of Jerusalem

Around the middle of the fourth century, Saint Cyril of Jerusalem pened these lines: "Do not see in the bread and wine merely natural elements, because the Lord has expressly said that they are his body and his blood: faith assures you of this, though your senses suggest otherwise".[7] While the Church's teaching on the Real Presence goes back to Yeshua himself, it is clear that Protestants were not the first ones to challenge it. Cyril countered those who argued that the bread and wine were merely natural elements by appealing to faith because our senses cannot make out the difference between ordinary bread and wine and the consecrated elements. All that has been argued here is to be accepted on faith, and such faith is actually a gift of God, who has to enable our faith.

These words were written centuries before the notion of "transubstantiation" was developed to explain the Real Presence in the Medieval era.[8] Other Church Fathers such as Origen agreed.

5. McGonigle and Quigley, *Tradition*, 76–77.

6. CCC §1457.

7. Cyril of Jerusalem, *Mystagogical catecheses*, 22:6.

8. Barron, *Eucharist*, 80–98; see also Horn, *Case*; Howell, *Eucharist*.

Origen of Alexandria

Though declared a heretic on other topics, Origen of Alexandria attests poignantly to the Real Presence in the Eucharist in expressing the care one must have for the consecrated element, namely Yeshua:

> You are accustomed to take part in the divine mysteries, so you know how, when you have received the body of the Lord, you reverently exercise every care lest a particle of it fall, and lest anything of the consecrated gift perish... how is it that you think neglecting the word of God a lesser crime than neglecting his body?[9]

This clearly presupposes the Real Presence.

Gregory of Nyssa

In the fourth century CE, Gregory of Nyssa, Bishop in Cappadocia, wrote:

> Rightly then, do we believe that the bread consecrated by the word of God has been made over into the Body of the God the Word. For that Body was, as to its potency bread; but it has been consecrated by the lodging there of the Word, who pitched His tent in the flesh.[10]

Gregory also explained that "The bread again is at first common bread, but when the sacramental action consecrates it, it is called, and becomes, the Body of Christ."[11]

The list of Church Fathers attesting to the Real Presence of Christ in the Eucharist as the uniform belief of the Church could go on, but for brevity's sake and in light of the numerous volumes that have already treaded this well-worn path, let us proceed.

---

9. Origen, *Homilies on Exodus*, 13:3.
10. Gregory of Nyssa, *Great Catechism*, 37:9–13.
11. Gregory of Nyssa, *In Diem Luminum*, 225.

Eucharistic Adoration

Although intellectually assenting to or believing in Eucharistic miracles is not a requirement of the faith, they should give one pause, for they are edifying and transformative for many. Countless stories surround them, in the lives of the saints as well as in the lives of our contemporaries.[1] From students and psychotherapy clients, I hear numerous cases of miraculous events occurring at Mass or at Adoration. If the Eucharist indeed makes our Savior present in us, no wonder the transformative power of the Eucharist results in Eucharistic miracles that baffle scientists. Understanding the Eucharist as the sacrifice of Jesus is the basis for the objective power at Adoration since a sacrifice is meant to transform something, in this case us. On this basis, no wonder the transformation occurs, even if it is not always clearly perceptible to our senses because we are finite beings.

Adoration of the Eucharist is when the host is exposed before us for veneration outside the Mass, usually in a chapel dedicated to this practice. Although God is present everywhere ("omnipresent"), the monstrance of the Blessed Sacrament in a dedicated space helps us focus on God's presence in a special way. In other words, our presence in the Adoration chapel facilitates our access to the Real Presence in ways that differ from praying at home or elsewhere, with the exception of the Mass. Many report experiencing more of a sense of peace while at Adoration, whether Catholics or not. Is it any wonder then that many

1. Cruz, *Miracles.*

a Catholic have made Adoration one of the centerpieces of their spirituality, such as the brilliant intellectual and convert, Saint Edith Stein, martyred at Auschwitz.

As noted in the Introduction, Thomas Aquinas credits his great ideas to laying his head upon the tabernacle that housed the Eucharist, as opposed to his own intellect. There is no superstition in this. It is simply the consequence of our ability to make us ready to encounter God who waits for those moments to act and dispense his grace. It is not our actions that make God act. God acts all the time and it is our effort to make us receptive that allows us to benefit from His works.

How God acts is specific to each one of us. Though as therapist I am privy to many reports from clients, the aim here is not to list concrete examples of Eucharistic miracles. These miracles belong to the sacred intimacy of each one of us. Listing them would either be trite or voyeurist. Eucharistic miracles are part and parcel of the greatest miracle of all, the fact that we are alive to experience what makes life miraculous, i.e., the daily miracles that we take for granted as long as no crisis intervenes to make us count our blessings.

No wonder then, that healings are associated with the practice of Eucharist Adoration. Just as with Mass, sometimes at Adoration God gives us his grace and we leap forward more so than normal. Like attending Mass, Adoration takes discipline. We exercise the body, so too do we train our souls. Adoration is one such practice that provides huge benefits.

Though Adoration or belief in Eucharistic miracles are no requirement of the faith, Eucharistic Adoration as much as partaking in Mass are nothing less than an encounter with Christ in the present of our passing life. These practices are best done for themselves rather than to obtain miracles. The ensuing miracles are from the grace of God given to us in the Sacrament of the Holy Eucharist, not as rewards, but as the fruits of a healthy life rooted in the presence of Jesus.

Conclusion

From Yeshua's time when he walked first-century Palestine through the beginning of the Church and onto the Church Fathers, the Medieval era right up to today, the Real Presence of Yeshua in the Eucharist has been the consistent teaching of the Church. The Protestant notion that it needs to be understood symbolically had precedents in earlier times as is obvious from the writings of Cyril. Martin Luther himself was comfortable with the Catholic Eucharist understanding. It was not until the second-generation reformers in the sixteenth century that Protestants began to challenge it. That they could not come up with a single understanding among themselves reveals the difficulties involved in going against fifteen centuries of Church teaching. But going against the biblical texts discussed above is even more damning for the various shades of Protestantism that insist so much on the primacy of Scripture (*"sola scriptura"*).

In fact, the Protestant arguments against the Real Presence of Christ in the Eucharist are not based on Scripture but on philosophical categories that arose in the modern era. In Antiquity until Aquinas, bread and wine could be flesh and blood while continuing to look and taste like bread and wine. There was no scientific objection to such a phenomena until Aristotle's philosophical tenets were challenged in the early modern era. Therefore, Protestant arguments against the Real Presence are a matter of philosophy and the way the physical world is conceived, not a matter of biblical interpretation.

Does this mean that the rise of new philosophical categories invalidates the biblical, Orthodox and Catholic understandings of the Eucharist as the "sacrament of our salvation accomplished by Christ on the cross"?[1] Not at all! It simply means that the elements of the Eucharist are supernatural, something reminiscent to Jerome's rendering of the so-called "daily bread" all Christians pray for as super-substantial bread.

As such, the Eucharist retains all its validity as medicine and healing balm in our hurting world. There are indeed other ways to transform one's life, but the Eucharist is one of them, besides the other sacraments that the Church has faithfully handed out to humanity for the last twenty centuries.

Today, the modern philosophies that rendered Aristotalien categories obsolete have become obsolete themselves. Does this mean that post-modern philosophical categories render the biblical, Orthodox, and Catholic understanding of the Eucharist doubly invalid? Not at all! As super-substantial bread, the Eucharist evolves in a reality beyond the reach of subatomic physics. The medicine of the Eucharist cannot be submitted to chemical analysis anymore than the work effected in psychotherapy. Yet, both generate changes that are undeniable.

My hope is to have made the reader reflect on the mystery of the faith and its paramount sacrament. The Eucharist has the power to transform and is truly grace, the grace of Christ that comes to us and in us. Staying away from the Eucharist is missing out on the fullness of the faith. Grace, food for the hard journey of life, spiritual healing and transformation, sometimes physical as well, and the forgiveness of venial sins[2] all flow from partaking of Jesus regularly as he commanded in Scripture.

The Temple of Bread gives us the bread of life for our subsistence. The Eucharist is the greatest mystery in the history of the world hiding in plain sight. How Christ and his Church wish the veil before individuals' eyes would be lifted to see this truth! This is actually the most important news in the history of our world.

1. CCC §1359.
2. CCC §1393–94.

The two questions presented at the outset remain: Who do you say that I am? and What is the Eucharist? The short answer is our Savior and Yeshua. He was born in Bethlehem, the Temple of Bread, and is the bread we pray for daily, not simply to sustain our bodies—which is naturally a prerequisite—but also our entire being—body and soul. Scripture and Tradition affirm what the Church has always maintained—that the body, blood, soul, and divinity of Yeshua are really, truly, and substantially present in the Blessed Sacrament of the altar. This Holy Mystery is waiting for you. Praise be to our Lord Yeshua the Christ who provides for us and comes to us in the Blessed Sacrament. May we all humbly approach and meet Yeshua in the Sacrament.

Bibliography

Anderson, James S. "El, Yahweh and Elohim: The Evolution of God in Israel and Its Theological Implications." *The Expository Times* 128 (2017) 261–67.

———. *Extolling Yeshua*. Eugene, OR: Wipf & Stock, 2019.

———. *Monotheism and Yahweh's Appropriation of Baal*. New York: T. & T. Clark, 2015.

Barron, Robert. *Eucharist*. Park Ridge: Word on Fire, 2021.

Cabie, Robert. *History of the Mass*. Translated by Lawrence J. Johnson. Beltsville: Pastoral, 1992.

Cruz, Joan C. *Eucharistic Miracles and Eucharistic Phenomenon in the Lives of the Saints*. Rockford, IL: Tan, 1991.

Cyril of Jerusalem. *Mystagogical Catecheses*. https://www.ewtn.com/catholicism/library/catechetical-lectures-1323-incl-mystagogical-catecheses-9085

Francis, Pope. *Amoris Laetitia: On Love in the Family*. Huntingdon: IN: Our Sunday Visitor, 2016.

———. *Evangelii Gaudium* [*The Joy of the Gospel*]. https://www.vatican.va/content/francesco/en/apost_exhortations/documents/papa-francesco_esortazione-ap_20131124_evangelii-gaudium.htm.

Gallagher, Timothy M. *Discerning the Will of God: An Ignatian Guide to Christian Decision Making*. New York: Crossroad, 2009.

Gregory of Nyssa. *Great Catechism*. http://www.mercyuponall.org/wp-content/uploads/2016/06/1819-1893_Schaff._Philip_3_Vol_05_Gregory_Of_Nyssa_EN.pdf.

———. *In Diem Luminum*. https://nftu.net/sermon-day-lights-st-gregory-nyssa/.

Hahn, Scott. *The Fourth Cup: Unveiling The Mystery of the Last Supper and the Cross*. New York: Crown, 2018.

———. *The Lamb's Supper: The Mass as Heaven on Earth*. New York: Doubleday, 1999.

Heschmeyer, Joe. *The Early Church Was the Catholic Church*. San Diego: Catholic Answers, 2021.

Horn, Trent. *The Case for Catholicism: Answers to Classic and Contemporary Protestant Objections*. San Francisco: Ignatius, 2017.

Howell, Kenneth J. *The Eucharist for Beginners: Sacrament, Sacrifice, and Communion.* San Diego: Catholic Answers, 2006.

Klawans, Jonathan. "Was Jesus' Last Supper a Seder?" *Bible Review* (October 2001) 24–47.

Levering, Matthew, and Michael Dauphinais. *The Wisdom of the Word: Biblical Answers to Ten Pressing Questions about Catholicism.* Park Ridge, IL: Word on Fire, 2021.

Madrid, Patrick. *Why Be Catholic: Ten Answers to a Very Important Question.* New York: Image, 2014.

Martin, Sean S. *American Pope: Scott Hahn and the Rise of Catholic Fundamentalism.* Eugene, OR: Wipf & Stock, 2021.

McGonigle, Thomas D., and James F. Quigley. *A History of the Christian Tradition: From Its Jewish Origins to the Reformation.* New York: Paulist, 1988.

O'Conner, James T. *The Hidden Manna: A Theology of the Eucharist.* 2nd ed. San Francisco: Ignatius, 2005.

Pitre, Brant. *Jesus and the Jewish Roots of the Eucharist: Unlocking the Secrets of the Last Supper.* New York: Doubleday, 2011.

Radcliffe, Timothy. *Why Go to Church? The Drama of the Eucharist.* London: Black, 2009.

Ray, Stephen K. *Crossing the Tiber: Evangelical Protestants Discover the Historical Church.* San Francisco: Ignatius, 1997.

Schuchts, Bob. *Be Healed: A Guide to Encountering the Powerful Love of Jesus in Your Life.* Notre Dame, IN: Ave Maria, 2014.

Sandnes, Karl O. "Jesus' Last Meal according to Mark." In *The Eucharist—Its Origins and Contexts,* edited by David Hellholm and Dieter Sänger, 453–75. Tübingen: Mohr Siebeck, 2017.

Sri, Edward. *A Biblical Walk through the Mass: Understanding What We Say and Do in the Liturgy.* West Chester: Ascension, 2014.

Vatican II. "Dei Verbum." In *The Conciliar and Post Conciliar Documents,* edited by Austin Flannery. Collegeville, MN: Liturgical, 1975. https://www.vatican.va/archive/hist_councils/ii_vatican_council/documents/vat-ii_const_19651118_dei-verbum_en.html

———. "Lumen Gentium." In Vatican Council II: The Conciliar and Post Conciliar Documents, edited by Austin Flannery, 1–96. Collegeville, MN: Liturgical, 1975. https://www.vatican.va/archive/hist_councils/ii_vatican_council/documents/vat-ii_const_19641121_lumen-gentium_en.html

———. "Nostra Aetate." In *The Conciliar and Post Conciliar Documents,* edited by Austin Flannery. Collegeville, MN: Liturgical, 1975. https://www.vatican.va/archive/hist_councils/ii_vatican_council/documents/vat-ii_decl_19651028_nostra-aetate_en.html